THEN AND NOW

TOYS AND GAMES

Bobbie Kalman

LIGHTBOX
openlightbox.com

Go to **www.openlightbox.com** and enter this book's unique code.

ACCESS CODE

LBXZ3583

Lightbox is an all-inclusive digital solution for the teaching and learning of curriculum topics in an original, groundbreaking way. Lightbox is based on National Curriculum Standards.

LIGHTBOX SUPPLEMENTARY RESOURCES

SHARE
Share titles within your Learning Management System (LMS) or Library Circulation System

CURRICULUM
Find national and state curriculum correlations

CITATION
Create bibliographical references following the Chicago Manual of Style

STANDARD FEATURES OF LIGHTBOX

AUDIO High-quality narration using text-to-speech system

ACTIVITIES Printable PDFs that can be emailed and graded

SLIDESHOWS Pictorial overviews of key concepts

VIDEOS Embedded high-definition video clips

WEBLINKS Curated links to external, child-safe resources

TRANSPARENCIES Step-by-step layering of maps, diagrams, charts, and timelines

INTERACTIVE MAPS Interactive maps and aerial satellite imagery

QUIZZES Ten multiple-choice questions that are automatically graded and emailed for teacher assessment

KEY WORDS Matching key concepts to their definitions

This title is part of our Lightbox digital subscription

Lightbox Grades 3–5 Subscription
ISBN 978-1-5105-5424-5

Access hundreds of Lightbox titles with our digital subscription. Sign up for a **FREE** subscription trial at **www.openlightbox.com/trial**

THEN AND NOW

TOYS AND GAMES

Contents

Long Ago and Today

Children today have a choice of many toys and games. They play with toys and games for fun, but they can also learn skills, such as reading and writing, while they play. Children play at home, at school, and outdoors.

Some toys, such as spinning hoops, are great exercise.

Favorite Toys ?

What are your favorite toys and games? Why do you like them?

During work parties, bundles of hay created good opportunities for children to play.

How Did They Play?

Long ago, there were few toys and no video games. Children also had less time to play because they had to help their parents work on the farm or around the house. Children still had fun playing, however. At work parties called bees, they played with the other children after they helped their parents work.

Popular Toys

Today, children have a lot of time to play. Each year, new kinds of toys are made for them to enjoy. Many of the new toys are similar to the kinds of toys their parents and grandparents played with long ago.

Toys from the Past

Popular toys in the past were dolls, doll houses, building blocks, and a toy called Noah's **Ark**. The toy was based on a Bible story in which Noah built an ark, or giant boat, because a great flood was coming. Noah took two of every kind of animal on the boat. The Noah's Ark toy had several animals.

Toys Then and Now

Ask your grandparents what toys they played with when they were kids. Which of their toys were the same as or similar to yours?

The first teddy bears were made of real fur. Today, they are made of different types of fuzzy fabric.

Construction blocks made from wood were a popular toy in the past. Today, they are still a favorite toy of young children.

In the past, only toys based on Bible stories, such as Noah's Ark, were allowed on Sundays.

Dolls in the past were made from wood, china, or fabric. Today, dolls are often made from plastic.

Old-fashioned skipping ropes had wooden handles. Some skipping ropes still have wooden handles today.

Toys with Power

Many toys today are powered by batteries or electricity. Some have **remote controls**. Children use remote controls to make helicopters fly, give robots directions, or play video games. Which of your toys have remote controls?

How Did These Toys Move?

Long ago, people did not have electricity, batteries, or remote controls. Some toys were wound like clocks. That is why they were called **clockwork toys**. Small wheels inside the toys helped them move for a short time.

In jack-in-the-box toys, turning a crank makes the toy play music. A spring makes the toy pop up outside the box.

Toy Timeline

Toys have existed for centuries. Early toys were simple and made of common materials. Toys have become more complex in recent years.

Children in ancient Rome play with dolls made of different materials, such as bone or wood.

1762

The jigsaw puzzle is invented as a teaching tool. It is made by cutting a map into pieces.

1949

Lego construction blocks arrive on the market.

1959

The Barbie doll is launched in the United States.

1966–1968

American **engineer** Ralph Baer creates an early video game set known as "the Brown Box."

2021

More than 50 percent of U.S. households own one or more video game consoles.

Old Games Still Played

There are many kinds of word and number games that have been played by children for hundreds of years. Dominoes, **anagrams**, and other games are still fun to play.

Board games

Games such as Snakes and Ladders, checkers, and chess are very old board games. Which ones do you like to play?

Chess is played by two players. Each player has 16 pieces. Players try to capture each other's pieces by moving their own pieces according to specific rules.

BOARD GAMES AROUND THE WORLD

GO
Invented in China
Around 2000 BC

SENET
Invented in Egypt
Around 3000 BC

PACHISI
Invented in India
4th Century AD

STERNHALMA
Invented in Germany
1892

An abacus can help young children learn how to add and subtract.

Classroom Games

Long ago, the main subjects taught in school were language arts and math. These are also some of the main subjects taught today. There are many games that help teach these subjects to children. Some of these games can be played on **digital tablets** and **smartphones**.

Fun to Learn

Long ago, children who lived in the country went to one-room schools. Children of all ages were taught in the same classroom by one teacher. There were not many school supplies, so the teacher used games and simple tools, such as **abacuses**, to make learning fun.

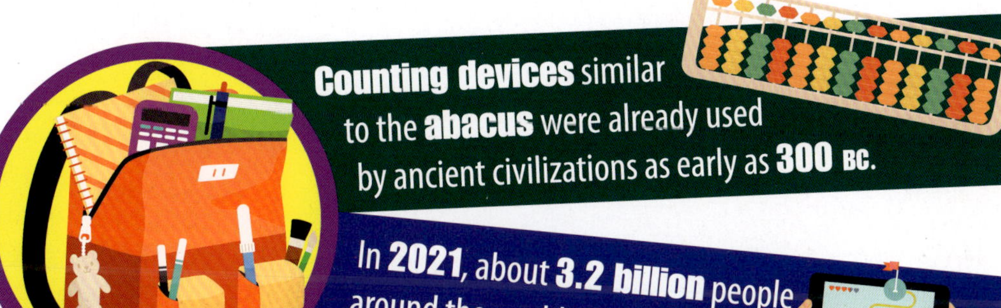

Outdoor Fun

Several popular outdoor games of the past are still played today. This is because many of these games can be played with little equipment. For instance, the game of tug-of-war only requires a rope to be played.

How Did They Play?

Leapfrog and Sardines were two popular games. To play leapfrog, the players line up behind one another and leap over the person in front. In Sardines, one person hides, while the rest, called seekers, count. When a seeker finds the hider, they both hide in the same place. Eventually, everyone except the last seeker is in the same hiding place.

The goal of tug-of-war is to pull the opposing team over a line on the ground.

Sports Then and Now

Many of the sports that are played today are like the sports played long ago. Baseball became a common sport in the 1850s. Football also became popular in the 1800s. Other sports played then and now are badminton, hockey, and lacrosse. Lacrosse was learned from Native Americans. It is still a very popular sport, especially in Canada.

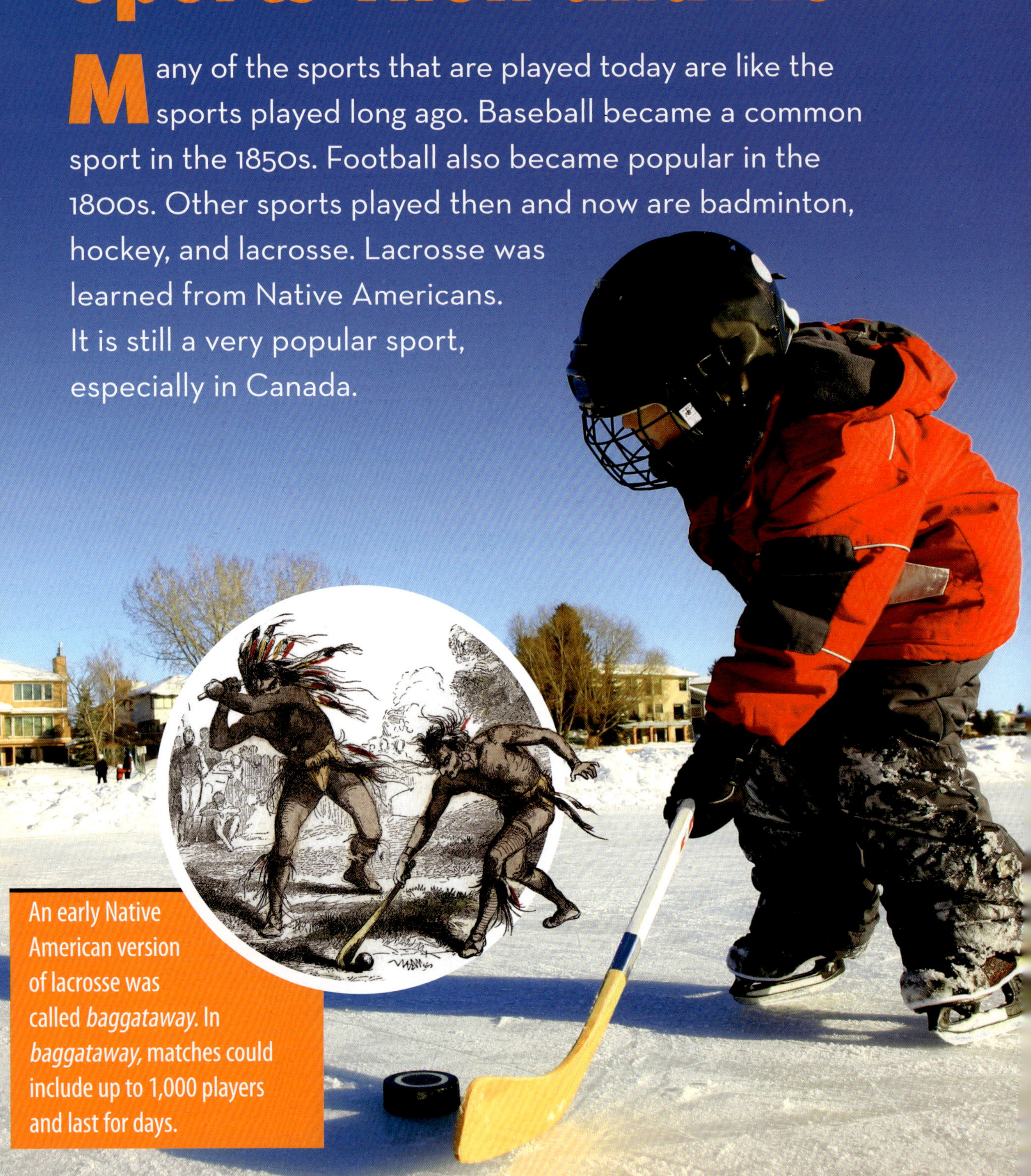

An early Native American version of lacrosse was called *baggataway*. In *baggataway*, matches could include up to 1,000 players and last for days.

Sports around the World

Many different kinds of sports were created around the world. Some sports are very ancient. Others were developed in recent times.

United States

Football is the most popular spectator sport in the United States. The sport was created in North America by combining elements of rugby and soccer. In the 1870s, players started carrying footballs instead of just kicking them.

Asia

Africa

Indian Ocean

Greece

Events similar to track and field have been practiced since ancient times. Greece is known for the ancient Olympic Games. These competitions were held in the city of Olympia for the first time in 776 BC and continued to be held for more than 11 centuries.

Malaysia

Played in southeast Asia since the 1400s, sepak takraw is the national sport of Malaysia. In sepak takraw, two teams, each made of three players, have to kick a small ball across a volleyball-like net without using their hands and arms.

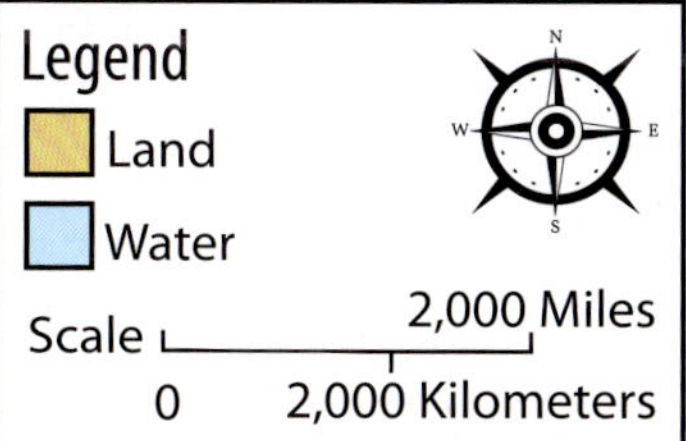

Rolling on Wheels

Rolling on wheels is great exercise! Scooters, skateboards, skates, and bicycles all have wheels. Many children enjoy the thrill of mountain biking, which takes them over rough areas without roads, such as hills.

It is important to wear safety equipment when practicing sports on wheels.

Bikes, Scooters, and Roller Skates

Many early bicycles had a huge front wheel. This kind of bike was called a ***velocipede***, which means "fast foot" in French. Very few children had bicycles because they were expensive. Instead, children rode scooters and also had roller skates. They could not ride skateboards because there were no skateboards until the 1950s.

Did You Know?

Skateboarding was started by surfers who wanted to "surf" on land when there were no waves in the ocean.

Velocipedes were very dangerous. The large wheel at the front made them unstable.

Scooters had long handlebars and a footboard with a wheel at each end.

Roller skates were strapped onto shoes.

Party and Holiday Games

People throw parties because they want to have fun with their family and friends. They hold parties to celebrate personal events, such as birthdays or weddings, and public and religious holidays.

A piñata is a decorated container that hangs from a rope and is filled with small toys and candy. Children take turns to hit it with a stick until it breaks.

Parties and Holidays Long Ago

People long ago gathered together with family and friends for the same reasons people gather today. At parties, children played many kinds of games, such as bobbing for apples. Apples float and bounce around in water, so biting into them without holding them is difficult. Bag and Stick was a popular game for Christmas parties. It was similar to breaking a piñata, which is a beloved party game that came from Mexico.

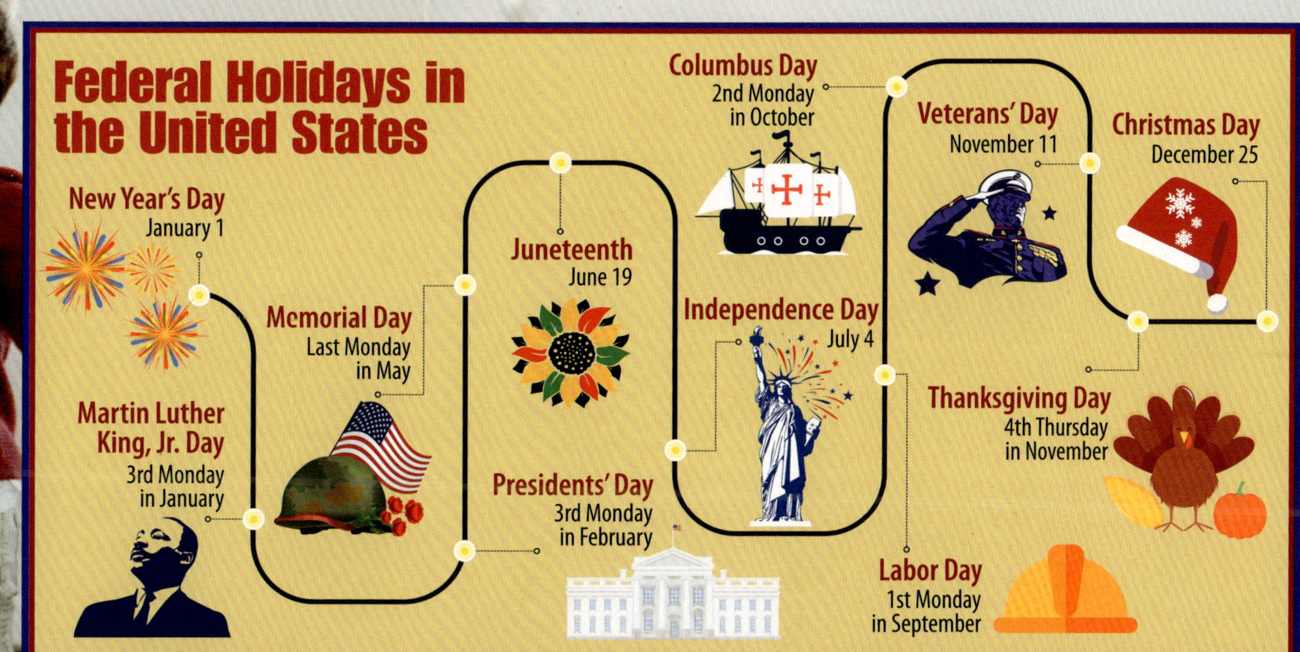

Quiz

1 When was the Barbie doll launched in the United States?

2 Sepak takraw is the national sport of which country?

3 When is Veterans' Day?

4 Why were velocipedes very dangerous?

5 Name three materials dolls were made from in the past.

6 What percentage of U.S. households owned one or more video game consoles in 2021?

7 What is the goal of tug-of-war?

8 Where was the game Sternhalma invented?

ANSWERS
1. In 1959 **2.** Malaysia
3. On November 11 **4.** Their large front wheel made them unstable.
5. Wood, china, and fabric
6. More than 50 percent **7.** To pull the opposing team over a line on the ground
8. In Germany

Key Words

abacuses: math tools with a wire frame containing beads that slide

anagrams: words or phrases created by rearranging the letters of other words and phrases

ark: a large boat from the Bible built by Noah to save himself, his family, and two of every kind of animal from a flood

clockwork toys: toys that are wound like a clock in order to run or carry out certain motions for a short time

digital tablets: portable computers that are operated by touching the screen

engineer: a person trained in how to build things and use different materials

remote controls: devices used to control a machine from a certain distance away

smartphones: cellphones that include some functions of computers

velocipede: an old bicycle with a large front wheel

Index

LIGHTBOX

SUPPLEMENTARY RESOURCES

Click on the plus icon ⊕ found in the bottom left corner of each spread to open additional teacher resources.

- Download and print the book's quizzes and activities
- Access curriculum correlations
- Explore additional web applications that enhance the Lightbox experience

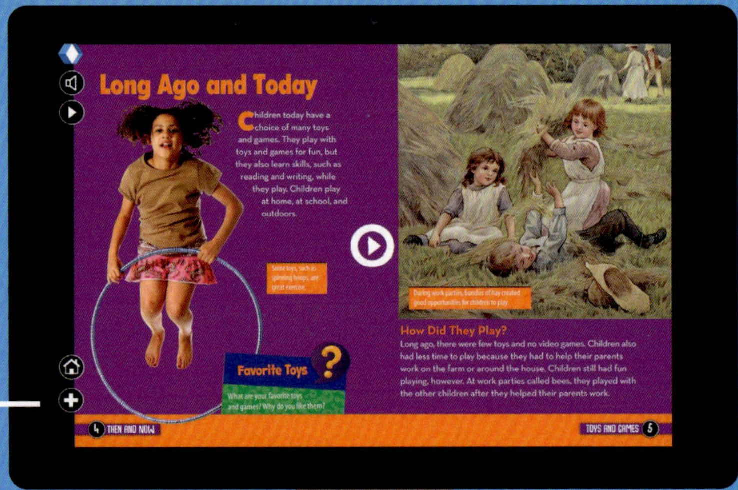

LIGHTBOX DIGITAL TITLES

Packed full of integrated media

VIDEOS

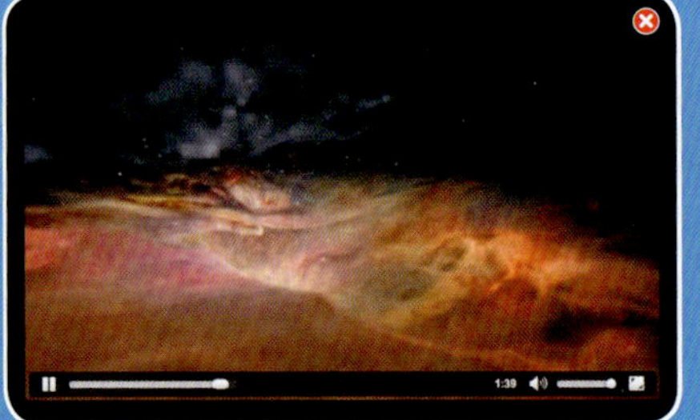

INTERACTIVE MAPS

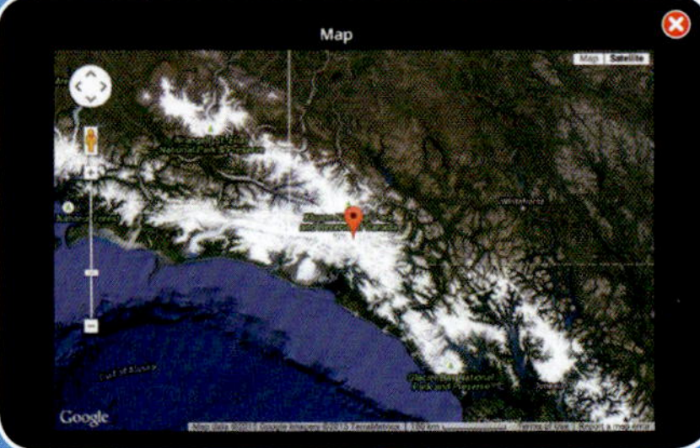

WEBLINKS

SLIDESHOWS

QUIZZES

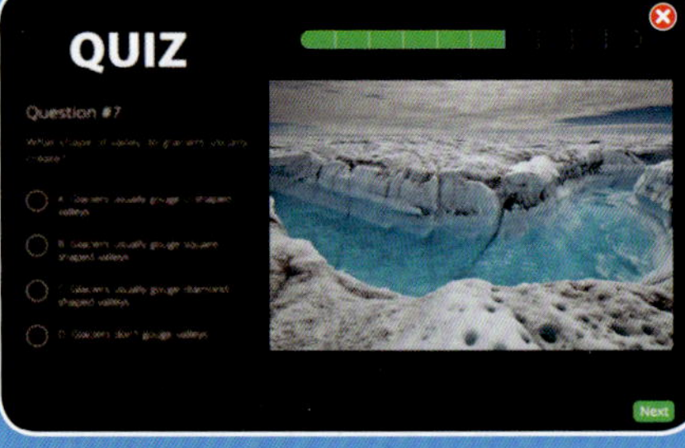

OPTIMIZED FOR

- ✓ TABLETS
- ✓ WHITEBOARDS
- ✓ COMPUTERS
- ✓ AND MUCH MORE!

Published by Lightbox Learning Inc.
276 5th Avenue, Suite 704 #917
New York, NY 10001
Website: www.openlightbox.com

First published by Crabtree Publishing Company in 2014

Library of Congress Control Number: 2020942131

ISBN 978-1-5105-5502-0 (hardcover)
ISBN 978-1-5105-5503-7 (multi-user eBook)

Printed in Guangzhou, China
1 2 3 4 5 6 7 8 9 0 26 25 24 23 22

102022
111021

Photo Credits
Every reasonable effort has been made to trace ownership and to obtain permission to reprint copyright material. The publisher would be pleased to have any errors or omissions brought to its attention so that they may be corrected in subsequent printings. The publisher acknowledges Alamy, Getty Images, Shutterstock, and Bridgeman Images as its primary image suppliers for this title.

Project Coordinator Sara Cucini
Designer Ana María Vidal